MODERN ROLE MO

Maria Sharapova

Kerrily Sapet

Mason Crest Publishers

Produced by OTTN Publishing in association with
21st Century Publishing and Communications, Inc.

MASON CREST PUBLISHERS INC.
370 Reed Road
Broomall, Pennsylvania 19008
(866) MCP-BOOK (toll free)
www.masoncrest.com

Printed in the United States of America.

First Printing

9 8 7 6 5 4 3 2 1

Library of Congress Cataloging-in-Publication Data

Sapet, Kerrily, 1972–
    Maria Sharapova / Kerrily Sapet.
        p. cm. — (Modern role models)
    Includes bibliographical references and index.
    ISBN-13: 978-1-4222-0490-0 (hardcover) — ISBN-13: 978-1-4222-0777-2 (pbk.)
    ISBN-10: 1-4222-0490-1 (hardcover)
    1.Sharapova, Maria, 1987–   —Juvenile literature. 2. Tennis players—Russia
(Federation)—Biography—Juvenile literature. 3. Women tennis players—Russia
(Federation)—Biography—Juvenile literature. I. Title.
GV994.S47S26 2009
796.342092—dc22
[B]   2008021355

Publisher's note:
All quotations in this book come from original sources, and contain the spelling and grammatical inconsistencies of the original text.

CROSS-CURRENTS

In the ebb and flow of the currents of life we are each influenced by many people, places, and events that we directly experience or have learned about. Throughout the chapters of this book you will come across **CROSS-CURRENTS** reference boxes. These boxes direct you to a **CROSS-CURRENTS** section in the back of the book that contains fascinating and informative sidebars and related pictures. Go on. ▸▸

CONTENTS

Maria Sharapova has found fame on the tennis court for overpowering her opponents with her powerful backhand. But she is also well known for her ability to sport some serious fashion. The Russian-born tennis star is celebrated for her style and glamour off the court as well as for her talent and determination on the court.

An Unexpected Champion

MARIA SHARAPOVA, ONE OF THE MOST RECOG- nized athletes in the world, ranks among the best professional women's tennis players today. The talented athlete has won more than 25 professional championship titles and received numerous awards in the course of her career. She's the first Russian to be ranked number one in the world.

Maria is also one of the world's wealthiest female athletes. In her career, she has earned nearly $12 million in **tournament** prize money. And she's made much more than that by **endorsing** products with various corporations. Despite her money and fame, Maria stays focused on the sport she has loved all of her life.

⫸ A RISING STAR ⫷

From a young age Maria made success her goal. She dedicated herself to tennis, practicing intensely every day and giving herself little time for family and friends. Her trainer, Nick Bollettieri, once said:

> **"She is extremely strict, disciplined, and a perfectionist. She plays tennis like she's preparing for an attack, a battle. That's Maria Sharapova. There is no monkey business. Every shot has a purpose. She runs for every single, solitary ball. Yeah, she'll smile, but it's . . . business."**

In women's professional tennis, players are ranked by the Women's Tennis Association (WTA), which is the main organizing body for the sport. At the end of 2002, soon after Maria became a professional, her WTA world ranking in **singles** tennis was 186. Within a year, Maria had battled her way to reach the number 32 spot. By late June 2004, Maria was ranked at number 15, but still relatively unknown when she stepped out onto the grass courts at the prestigious tennis tournament at Wimbledon. Few people in the tennis world considered the 17-year-old a serious threat to the top athletes competing there.

CROSS-CURRENTS

If you'd like to find out how pro tennis events are organized, check out "The Women's Tennis Association." Go to page 50. ▶▶

⫸ FACING THE COMPETITION ⫷

Held each year in London, Wimbledon is one of the four major tournaments of tennis known as the **Grand Slam** events. Players consider winning at Wimbledon to be one of the ultimate tennis achievements.

CROSS-CURRENTS

To learn more about the most important tennis events held each year, read "Grand Slam Tournaments." Go to page 51. ▶▶

The tournament consists of a series of tennis matches that take place over the course of two weeks. The women's singles tournament starts with a field of 128 players. Those who win their matches advance to the next round. The field of players is reduced to 64 after the first round, to 32 after the second round, to 16 after the third round, to 8 in the quarterfinals, to 4 in the semifinals, and then 2 in the final. The winner of the final is crowned the champion.

As the 2004 Wimbledon tournament got underway in late June, Maria steadily advanced, swiftly defeating her early competitors

At age 16 Maria debuted at her first U.S. Open in 2003. In the first round of the tournament, which takes place in Flushing Meadows, New York, she handily defeated Virginia Ruano Pascual of Spain in a singles match held on August 25. Maria's determination was obvious. A reporter for *Sports Illustrated* noted: "This is a player who means business."

and reaching the quarterfinals. In this match, against Japanese star Ai Sugiyama, Maria fell behind early. However, she rallied to win.

The victory moved Maria into the semifinals, where she faced Lindsay Davenport. An American tennis star, Davenport had won Wimbledon in 1999 and was one of the highest-ranked players in the world. In this game, too, Maria trailed at first. But then the 17-year-old battled back fiercely to win the match and reach the final.

Maria's **opponent** in the Wimbledon final was U.S. player Serena Williams, who was heavily favored to win. The 22-year-old had won the previous two tournaments at Wimbledon. And she was the top-**seeded** player in the 2004 tournament. To many people in the crowd, Williams seemed invincible.

However, Maria was confident of her abilities. Once, when asked by reporters about whether she felt pressured to win a Grand Slam tournament, she had replied:

> **"It's a little early, but there is no pressure because there's excitement in me, there's a drive that I want to achieve that and nothing is going to stop me."**

➤ A GLORIOUS VICTORY ◄

On July 3, 2004, Maria walked onto the Wimbledon court for the final match, in front of nearly 14,000 spectators and millions of television viewers. She would later admit that she had felt some jitters before the match but her confidence soon returned.

In fact, Maria dominated, rocketing the ball past Williams and smashing it into the far corners of the court. Focused and intense, Maria quickly took the lead. Her **serves** reached a blistering 115 miles per hour. Williams struggled, making errors and failing to return Maria's serves effectively. In a little over an hour, Maria had won the match, defeating Williams in straight sets, 6-1, 6-4.

The victory ceremony was delayed for a few moments as television cameras captured Maria trying to call her mother with her cell phone to share the news. Finally, Maria was presented with the Wimbledon trophy—an ornate silver and gold tray known as the Venus Rosewater Dish. She also won $1 million in prize money. As Maria held the trophy, she apologized to Williams for taking it away from her for the year, adding that she hoped they would play many more times.

Afterwards, Maria climbed into the stands to find her father—who has also been her coach of many years. The two kissed and hugged. Later, she explained how much she appreciated her father:

> **"All that has happened in my life, all the tough moments we've been through, all the good moments. This is what I wanted to achieve all my life, and it happened. That's the person I wanted to share it with."**

Maria kisses the winner's trophy in front of a cheering crowd at Wimbledon. On July 3, 2004, the 17-year-old Russian won the women's singles final of the Grand Slam event, held in London, England. Maria, seeded at number 13, earned her first Grand Slam title by defeating number one seed Serena Williams of the United States.

Winning Wimbledon at 17 years old made Maria Sharapova an overnight celebrity. Her victory would be the first of many for the teenager, and it gave the tennis world a taste of what was to come from this talented young athlete.

The road to tennis fame started at age four for Maria. She and her family were living in the resort town of Sochi, Russia, when she first picked up a tennis racket. After seeing their daughter's natural ability, the Sharapovs decided to leave their native country so that Maria could train at the Nick Bollettieri Tennis Academy in the United States.

2

The Road to Tennis Fame

MARIA SHARAPOVA WAS BORN ON APRIL 19, 1987, to Yuri Sharapov (the masculine form of the Russian name) and Yelena Sharapova in the town of Nyagan, which was then part of the Soviet Union. Nyagan is an oil and gas industrial center in the western part of Siberia, a vast region that makes up much of northern Asia.

The Sharapovs had moved to Nyagan because of a terrible accident that occurred about a year before Maria was born. In 1986, the Sharapovs had been living in Gomel, a city in the former Soviet Union. On April 26, an explosion at the Chernobyl nuclear power plant, located about 80 miles (130 kilometers) away, caused harmful radiation to drift downwind to Gomel. Concerned about the risk to their health, Yuri and Yelena Sharapov fled thousands of miles east to Nyagan. There, Yuri worked in the nearby oil fields, while Yelena attended college.

CROSS-CURRENTS
If you would like more information about the tragic nuclear meltdown at Chernobyl, read "Disaster in Russia." Go to page 51. ▶▶

➣ AN EARLY TALENT ➤

Two years after Maria was born, her family moved to Sochi, a resort town bordering the Black Sea, in southern Russia. Maria's father, Yuri, enjoyed tennis, and Maria liked to watch him play. One of Yuri's friends was the father of Yevgeny Kafelnikov, a Russian tennis star. When Maria was four years old, Kafelnikov's father gave her an old tennis racket. Maria practiced hitting tennis balls against a wall at the park each day. She quickly grew to love the game.

In October 1993, when Maria was six, her father took her to a tennis clinic in Moscow. Martina Navratilova, an international tennis star from the Czech Republic, saw Maria playing. Navratilova suggested that the young girl begin training professionally at the world-renowned Nick Bollettieri Tennis Academy in Bradenton, Florida. Maria's parents soon began planning to move again.

➣ A NEW COUNTRY ➤

The following March, Maria and her father arrived in Florida. Neither of them spoke English. Both sets of Maria's grandparents had funded the trip, but Yuri had less than $700 in his pocket. Because she had difficulties obtaining a visa to enter the United States, Yelena Sharapova stayed behind. Years later, Maria recalled her feelings about being separated from her mother:

> **In those days I barely talked to her on the phone. You didn't really have good communication back then. I mean, we talked maybe once in six months. . . . But I always remember writing her letters. . . . I was just so excited and overwhelmed by the move to the United States, by the new surroundings.**

When Maria and her father arrived at the tennis academy, they were told that she was too young to enroll in the program. For the next two years, life was hard. Maria and her father settled in the nearby town of Venice. To support them, Yuri found odd jobs working in construction and driving a taxi. When he found time, he also coached Maria on local tennis courts.

➣ TRAINING BEGINS ➤

In December 1995, Maria and her father returned to the Nick Bollettieri

Sports Illustrated

JUNE 18, 1984 $1.95

IN A ZONE OF HER OWN

Martina Was Out Of This World In Paris

In late 1993, after tennis great Martina Navratilova saw six-year-old Maria play at a tennis clinic in Moscow, she advised Maria's father to enter the young girl in a tennis school. Navratilova, shown here on the cover of the June 1984 issue of *Sports Illustrated*, dominated women's professional tennis from the 1970s to the 2000s.

Tennis Academy. After watching her play for just five minutes, officials from International Management Group (IMG), a professional sports management company that owns the academy, offered Maria a **scholarship** of $46,000 a year. This covered the costs of training, tutoring, and living in the academy's dormitories.

In the academy dorms, nine-year-old Maria shared a room with three sixteen-year-old girls. She was skinny and quiet, and she didn't speak English well, so the older girls teased her. But Maria quickly picked up English and learned self-reliance.

In June 1996, Yelena Sharapova obtained the visa that allowed her to live in the United States. Maria was reunited with her mother, and the family moved into an apartment in Bradenton. Aside from attending some high-school level classes for a couple of years at the Pendleton School, which was associated with the academy, Maria would be home-schooled by her mother, who would also teach her about Russian culture.

⇒ THE YOUNG CHALLENGER ⇐

At 11 years old, Maria began training with tennis coach Robert Lansdorp, who was based in Los Angeles, California. She was also training with Nick Bollettieri, so she had to travel periodically from Florida to California to work with both coaches. Lansdorp described her ability at the time:

> **❝None of the things she did with a racquet impressed me all that much, but what I noticed right away was her intensity, coordination, and great tennis instincts. I knew if I could get her to focus and work hard, she could definitely have a future in this sport.❞**

With Lansdorp, Maria practiced for six hours every day. To help her make her **forehand** and **backhand** shots more precise, he sometimes placed targets, like empty tennis cans, on the court and told Maria to hit them. Maria also practiced making the tennis ball spin when she hit it. Spin makes the ball bounce in different ways, and makes it more difficult for opponents to return shots.

Maria is ambidextrous, meaning she can do things equally well with both her right and left hands. She experimented playing left-handed for a while, but around age 11 switched permanently to her right hand. However, being ambidextrous gives her an advantage because she can hit a shot

CROSS-CURRENTS

To learn more about how tennis is played and the basic rules of the sport, read "On the Court." Go to page 52. ▶▶

left-handed if she needs to. And being ambidextrous makes it easier to make backhand shots, too.

The International Management Group recognized that Maria was a star in the making. In April 1997, she signed an agreement to work with IMG. The following June, the promising young player also inked her first endorsement deal with Nike, a manufacturer of sports apparel and equipment.

Maria played in her first tournament at age 10, although she didn't win her first championship title until three years later. Thanks

Maria was nine years old when she enrolled at the Bollettieri Tennis Academy. By the following year she was competing in tournaments. On December 8, 1997, Maria entered her first major tournament—the Eddie Herr International Junior Championships as a wild card (when a player is unranked and has not had to participate in qualifying matches).

MARIA SHARAPOVA

to her intense training, Maria was soon beating older girls in junior tennis competitions.

➤ TURNING PRO ◄

On April 19, 2001, on her 14th birthday, Maria turned professional. She entered her first junior tennis professional tournament the same

Maria won the Eddie Herr International Junior Championship in December 2000, when she was 13 years old, while competing in the 16-and-under division. However, her official tennis career began in 2001, after she turned 14 and joined the junior circuit. That year she won 25 junior circuit matches and only lost three. In 2002, she had 26 victories and only three losses.

month. It was an International Tennis Federation event held in Sarasota, Florida, and she lost in the first round. She continued to compete in many more under-18 tournaments, winning many of them.

The following January, Maria played in the Australian Open Junior Championship, in Melbourne, where at age 14 she became the youngest player ever to reach the girl's singles finals. However, she was defeated in the final by 16-year-old Barbora Strycova of the Czech Republic.

In April 2002, Maria won her first professional title at an International Tennis Federation tournament in Gunma, Japan. She went on to win two subsequent ITF challenger events held that year—one in Vancouver, Canada, and the other in Peachtree City, Georgia. By the end of 2002, she had earned a WTA world ranking of 186.

In 2003, Maria continued to perform well. In fact, she debuted in all four Grand Slam tournaments. At Wimbledon, she advanced to the fourth round, becoming one of just sixteen remaining competitors, before losing to fellow Russian Svetlana Kuznetsova.

That October, Maria won her first WTA singles title at the Japan Open, held in Tokyo, and the **doubles** title as well. By the end of the season, Maria was ranked 32 by the WTA. She also received the WTA award for Newcomer of the Year in 2003.

Maria herself admitted feeling more confidence. She told reporters:

> **❝I definitely feel I belong. I go into tournaments thinking these are the people that are really scared of me. I can't go thinking I'm scared of them.❞**

➤ ENDORSEMENTS AND SPONSORS ◆

In advertising, it is common for a celebrity to promote a company's product in return for a negotiated fee. As various companies became aware of Maria's abilities, they offered to be her **sponsors**. In October 2002 she signed an endorsement deal with Prince, a company that manufactures tennis rackets. A year later, after her victory at the Japan Open, she agreed to endorse NEC Computers. That year, the blonde, blue-eyed rising star also signed a modeling contract with IMG Models.

In 2003 Maria had left the junior circuit, joined the WTA tour, and begun a quick rise in the women's singles world rankings. At the beginning of 2004, she was already ranked number 32. But many people would call 2004 her breakthrough year—when her Wimbledon Grand Slam win showed the world she was one of the best.

3

Becoming the Best

DESPITE MARIA'S SUCCESS IN 2003, FEW PEOPLE could have predicted how far she would go in the 2004 season. And few thought she would win a Grand Slam title. Determined to become the best, Maria had worked hard, building a reputation for the intensity and focus she brought to each match she played.

When not competing, Maria typically spends hours practicing each day, six days a week. Although practice has made her strong and powerful, Maria admits that she dislikes it. She has said:

> **"I don't love it, because I get impatient doing the same thing over and over. But I know there are things in my game that I can improve on. Preparation is what's going to help me be No. 1."**

⟫ WIMBLEDON RECORDS ⟪

In January, at the 2004 Australian Open, Maria had been knocked out in second round. The following June, at the French Open, in

Paris, she reached her first Grand Slam quarterfinal. But winning at Wimbledon in 2004 was an accomplishment that she didn't expect, she told reporters:

> **❝I never, never in my life expected this to happen so fast. It's always been my dream to come here and to win, but it was never in my mind that I would do it this year. ❞**

With that win, Maria became the first Russian tennis player ever to win that Grand Slam event. She was also the third-youngest female winner.

CROSS-CURRENTS

For more information on some of the best female tennis players in history, read "Tennis Greats." Go to page 53. ▶▶

Reporters noted another record that Maria achieved at Wimbledon. She had the habit of grunting and shrieking when she hit the ball. She now held the record for being the loudest player on Wimbledon's famous center court. Her yells reached 101.2 decibels, nearly as loud as a police siren. Some sports writers nicknamed her the Siberian Siren.

⇒ INSTANT FAME ⇐

The win at Wimbledon made Maria an instant celebrity. The next day, her father and Maria's IMG sports agents sat down with a calendar and plotted out her availability for working with corporate sponsors. Endorsement obligations were limited to three weeks a year so she could remain focused on tennis.

The endorsement offers poured in. The world had watched on television as Maria called her mother from the court at Wimbledon. By August, Maria had signed a $1 million global endorsement deal with the cell phone company Motorola. By the end of the year, she would sign deals with the soft drink manufacturer Pepsi; Honda, a car manufacturer; Canon, a camera company; and the Swiss company TAG Heuer, maker of luxury watches, phones, and eyewear.

Meanwhile, the media mobbed Maria with requests for interviews and photo shoots. Reporters and fans now examined every detail of the 17-year-old's life. Newspapers, magazines, Web sites, and chat rooms reported on her family and friends, her lifestyle, her food likes and dislikes, her clothes, and even her hobbies. In one

TAG Heuer was one of the many companies that signed up Maria shortly after her Grand Slam win at Wimbledon in 2004. In this advertisement for one of TAG Heuer's luxury watches, she appears as a celebrity "ambassador" for the Swiss company's "What are you made of?" campaign, which highlights the talents of celebrity athletes.

interview Maria mentioned that she had a stamp collection. The next day, stamp-collecting magazines and businesses flooded her agent with requests for interviews and endorsements.

⇒ BACK TO BUSINESS ⇐

After Wimbledon, some people wondered if Maria would play on the Russian team at the Summer Olympics being held that year in

Maria shows her determination as she struggles in her opening-round match against American player Laura Granvllle at the 2004 U.S. Open, in an August 31 match at Arthur Ashe Stadium in Flushing, New York. Although she made mistakes early on, Maria rallied and found the edge to defeat Granville 6-3, 5-7, 7-5.

Athens, Greece. However, the Olympics were only a month away, and the Russian team had already been selected when the Wimbledon tournament took place.

So Maria continued to compete at WTA tour events, losing early on in the U.S. Open, held in New York in September. But the following month, she won the Korea Open, held in Seoul. Later in October, she won the Japan Open, for the second year in a row. With that win, she celebrated her fourth WTA Tour singles title of 2004—and her ranking reached number seven.

Maria played her last tournament of the year in November, defeating Serena Williams a second time 4-6, 6-2, 6-4, at the WTA Championships, in Los Angeles, California. It had been a breakthrough season for Maria. Her achievements that year earned her two WTA awards—Player of the Year and Most Improved Player in 2004.

During the year, Maria had begun to work less with Lansdorp, who lived in California and rarely traveled. She had been hitting on a full-time basis with 30-year-old Michael Joyce, a former professional tennis player who had also trained with Lansdorp. Joyce soon assumed the role of part-time coach, traveling to tournaments with Maria and her father. However, Yuri remained Maria's official coach.

⇒ LIFE OF CELEBRITY ⇐

By the end of the year Maria had adapted to a new lifestyle. She was able to juggle training, tournaments, high school assignments, and commitments to sponsors who craved advertising time and photo opportunities. Her demanding travel schedule allowed little time for friends, family, or rest.

Some people have criticized Maria for spending too much time advertising products and attending her sponsors' special events. The tennis star insists that she keeps tennis her priority. However, she has acknowledged:

> **"There are definitely two Marias. There's the one who practices and grinds. And then there's the one you see on billboards. So what if I'm at one of these events? . . . I know that in two hours I'll be back in my room, in my pajamas, reading my book. . . . I've got to be ready for practice the next morning at 8."**

⇒ DONATING TO OTHERS ⇐

Along with her prize money from winning the WTA Championships in November, Maria received a Porsche Cayenne. She donated the value of the car (more than $56,000) to help people affected by a horrific massacre that occurred two months earlier in Russia. On September 1, a group of armed terrorists had taken nearly 1,000 children and teachers hostage at a school in the Russian town of Beslan. Three days later, when Russian troops stormed the building, explosions and fires had killed more than 300 of the hostages and injured hundreds more. Maria wanted the money to go to help the survivors and affected families recover from the tragedy.

That December, in another effort to help others, Maria participated in the WTA Tour's Hurricane Tennis Slam. Exhibition matches were held in Tampa, Florida, to raise money for the Florida Hurricane Relief Fund. The money went to helping communities with rebuilding efforts.

⇒ THE EARLY 2005 SEASON ⇐

Although Maria trained in the steamy heat of Florida, and at times on clay courts in sunny Spain, she suffered in the heat whenever she played at the Australian Open. Although it is held in January, the first Grand Slam tournament of the year occurs at the height of the summer because Australia is in the southern hemisphere. In 2005, the fierce Australian summer heat reached a baking 120°F on the synthetic rubber tennis courts.

Maria grimaced in the sun and sought shade between points during her quarterfinal match against Svetlana Kuznetsova. In the end, Maria won the match, and advanced to the semifinal, where she once again faced Serena Williams. Battling both the heat and fierce competition from Williams, Maria narrowly lost.

But Maria took charge in her next tournament. A week after the defeat in Australia, she beat Lindsay Davenport to win the Pan Pacific Open in Tokyo, Japan. In February, Maria took another championship title at the Qatar Total Open, in the capital city of Doha. Davenport came back at the Pacific Life Open in Indian Wells, California, where Maria lost to her in the semifinals. But then it was Maria's turn again, when at a tournament in Miami, she defeated Davenport and advanced to the final.

On a hot humid day in Key Biscayne, Florida, Maria stretches to return the ball to Marissa Irvin of the United States during the Nasdaq-100 Open. Sharapova won the match, which took place on March 27, 2005. The victory advanced her to the fourth round of the tournament, although she would lose in the final to Kim Clijsters of Belgium.

⇒ MORE ENDORSEMENTS ⇐

Later that spring, Maria signed several more endorsement deals. Her new sponsors included Colgate, a manufacturer of toothpaste and toothbrushes; Sega, Indie Built, and Digital Bridges, producers of video games; and Samantha Thavasa, a maker of jewelry and handbags. The previous year Maria had signed a contract with the perfume company Parlux, and created her own fragrance, called "Maria Sharapova," which launched in 2005.

In May 2005, Maria bought her first home, a $2.7 million house in Bradenton, Florida, where she planned to live with her parents. While Yuri traveled with Maria, her mother remained at home. She rarely attended tournaments, although she supported her daughter both on and off the court.

⇒ REACHING NUMBER ONE ⇐

In the middle of the 2005 season, Maria suffered a strained right pectoral muscle in her chest. This was the first significant injury she had to deal with. And it would hamper her play for the rest of

In December 2005, Maria was in Japan, where she played exhibition matches as part of the Maria Sharapova Japan Tour. The three-day tour consisted of matches played in the cities of Osaka, Nagoya, and Tokyo. On December 21, while she was in Osaka, she paid a visit to Osaka City General Hospital and presented Christmas gifts to hospitalized children.

the year. She still managed to play in five events, but withdrew from four others in order to rest.

Despite the injury, Maria's wins outnumbered her losses. She did so well that on August 22, 2005, the WTA ranked Maria number one in the world. A week later, she lost the honor to Lindsay Davenport, but regained the ranking in September. She then spent six more weeks at the top of the chart. Her former trainer Lansdorp has said:

> **Maria has this ability to just raise the level of her game, she can just defy everything and everybody. She'll be like, 'I don't give a hoot about anything' and go out and just play. She can get herself up to play the best tennis she can play because she wants to win so bad.**

During 2005, Maria met with many successes, despite her injury. She had won six tournaments since her victory at Wimbledon the previous year. And she had advanced to the quarterfinals at the French Open and reached the semifinals of three Grand Slams—the Australian Open, Wimbledon, and the U.S. Open.

⇛ To Russia and Japan ⇚

In October 2005, Maria traveled to Moscow, Russia, to participate for the first time in the WTA Tour event called the Kremlin Cup. To many Russians, Maria was a star returning home. Her fans, who called her Masha (the Russian nickname for Maria), considered her a Russian sports success story. Maria advanced to the quarterfinals of the women's singles tournament.

In December Maria played exhibition matches in Japan, as part of the Maria Sharapova Japan Tour. During the trip she starred in a fashion show, modeling jewelry she had designed. She also attended a children's tennis clinic and presented gifts to patients at the children's ward of Osaka City General Hospital.

Maria battles Daniela Hantuchova of Slovakia in this photograph from the Australian Tennis Open, in Melbourne. Maria's determination enabled her to defeat Hantuchova during the January 22, 2006, match and advance to the quarterfinals. Maria would have to fall back on her resolve and willpower in the months to come as injuries and emotional challenges would take their toll.

The Good and the Bad

IN JANUARY 2006, MARIA BEGAN HER WTA TOUR season in Melbourne at the Australian Open. Along with fierce competition, she again faced conditions that were difficult for her—the scorching sun and furnace-like courts. Still, Maria managed to make it to the semifinals, where she lost to Justine Henin-Hardenne of Belgium.

Shortly after her loss in Australia, Maria suffered another serious injury—a painful bone bruise on her right ankle. Her doctors recommended she take two months off from competing to allow the injury to heal.

⟫ UPS AND DOWNS ⟪

In March, Maria was ready to get back on the courts. She swiftly won the Pacific Life Open in California. Looking to continue that success, she competed next at the Nasdaq-100 Open in Miami, Florida.

CROSS-CURRENTS

Read "Aches and Pains" to learn about some common tennis injuries and how most players deal with them. Go to page 54. ▶▶

There, Maria played a controversial semifinal match against Tatiana Golovin of France. Maria won the first set of the match, but when Golovin started winning, Maria interrupted the set to take a bathroom break. The fans thought the behavior didn't show good **sportsmanship**, and they booed. After Golovin won the second set, Maria left the court again for the bathroom. Then, during the third set, Golovin hurt her left ankle. A hushed crowd watched as her coach taped up the injury. But the sprain was serious, and Golovin had to **forfeit** the match.

Usually, when a player is injured during a game, her opponent shows concern by checking with her. But Maria practiced her serve against the wall. Many onlookers criticized Maria for her behavior during and after the match. She would later say that she didn't realize Golovin's injury was serious and that she had needed the two breaks. In the tournament final, Maria lost to Svetlana Kuznetsova.

Although Maria's bone bruise had seemed to heal, two days before the French Open began on May 28, she aggravated the ankle during practice. A magnetic resonance imaging (MRI) scan confirmed that she was fit. She has said:

> **❝As long as the doctors give me an O.K., as long as I can play through the little aches and pains that I get from time on, then I'm O.K., I'm willing to do it. I take the good with the bad.❞**

With little preparation, Maria tackled the red clay courts of the French Open. She made it to the quarterfinals, where she lost to Russian Dinara Safina. But Maria proved to be a winner again a few months later, in September, by winning the Acura Classic in California. She could look back at her overall performance with satisfaction. In each of her past 26 tournaments, she had advanced to the quarterfinals or better.

⇒ A SECOND GRAND SLAM ⇐

In September 2006, Maria was well known at the U.S. Open in New York City—and everywhere else. Her image appeared on billboards and in television commercials. Since winning Wimbledon at age 17, the talented tennis star had become the highest-paid female athlete

DUBAI

Maria practices at Dubai Tennis Stadium on February 19, 2006, before the Dubai Women's Open. The presence of the 19-year-old tennis celebrity, who was competing at the event for the first time, drew a large audience. When the tournament final was played on February 25, Maria would lose to Justine Henin-Hardenne of Belgium.

in the world. *Forbes* magazine estimated her endorsement income at $19 million.

Fans attending the 2006 U.S. Open clamored at the fence to watch Maria practice. They gossiped about her possible romance with tennis player Andy Roddick. Many of them wondered if she could capture another Grand Slam title. Although she had won many tournaments, she had lost in five straight Grand Slam semifinals.

This time, Maria satisfied her fans. She won the semifinal and reached her first Grand Slam final in two years. She now faced Justine

Alicia Molik (in white) of Australia congratulates Maria for her win during the June 2006 French Open, held on the clay courts in Paris. The victory advanced Maria to the last 16 of the Grand Slam tournament, but she later lost in the quarterfinals to Russian Dinara Safina. Maria often struggles to win on clay, which she considers her least favorite surface.

Henin-Hardenne, who had defeated her four straight times since 2005. But at the end of the match, Maria triumphed, winning 6-4, 6-4. Thrilled to show that she could win another Grand Slam title, she dropped to her knees in joy. Later she said:

> **66When you go down on the ground, you just think of everything that you've put into this moment, and even though the moment is a very short time, you get to be on court with that trophy, it's just so incredible.99**

Maria returns the ball to Michaella Krajicek of the Netherlands during the first round of the 2006 U.S. Open Tennis Championships, in Flushing Meadows, New York. Sharapova won the match, 6-3, 6-0. She went on to claim the second Grand Slam title of her career with a victory over Justine Henin-Hardenne in the final.

⇒ CONTROVERSY ⇐

However, controversy surrounded Maria's win. Tennis officials don't allow coaching during a match. Many people believed Maria's father and Michael Joyce were illegally signaling Maria during her game against Henin-Hardenne. After the first set, Yuri held up a banana and Joyce was caught on camera flashing four fingers at her. When Yuri held up a water bottle, she drank water. Yuri explained that he and Joyce were just reminding Maria to eat and to have four drinks.

In the press conference held after the match, Maria told reporters she wanted to focus on her win, and not the controversy. She stated:

> **"I believe at the end of the day, personally, my life is not about a banana, it's not about what I wear, it's not about the friends that I have. My career right now is about winning a tennis match."**

Following Maria's win at the U.S. Open, she continued her streak. In October, she won tournaments in Switzerland and Austria, and made it to the semifinals of the WTA Championships.

⇒ TROUBLE IN 2007 ⇐

At the beginning of the 2007 season, the WTA ranked Maria number one in the world. She would remain on top for several weeks, despite having to deal with another serious injury. She had developed bursitis—a painful inflammation—in her right shoulder. Because it hurt to serve the ball, Maria became less accurate and less confident. And the need to rest her shoulder cut into her practice time.

Maria's shoulder bothered her during the 2007 Australian Open, where she nearly lost her opening match against Russian Vera Zvonareva. She faced more troubles when officials fined her father for illegal coaching during her quarterfinal against Anna Chakvetadze.

Even so, Maria advanced to the final, where she faced Serena Williams, the winner of the Australian Open in both 2003 and 2005. After an intense match, Williams beat Maria to win the title for a third time. Maria graciously congratulated Williams and then told the crowd:

Staying fit is important, especially for top athletes. To keep herself in shape, improve flexibility, and stay relaxed, Maria practices yoga—a discipline of using breath control, meditation, and body position to develop balance, stamina, and strength. Some tennis players rely on yoga to train the mind to relax and improve their concentration during matches.

"You can never underestimate [Williams] as an opponent. . . . She's an amazing champion, and she showed it here many times, and of course I look forward to playing her many more times, and winning a few, I hope."

Further injuries followed at Maria's next tournament game. At the Pan Pacific Open in Tokyo, she suffered a hamstring injury and strained her lower leg, which forced her to rest. One month later, and

In 2007 Maria went through several emotional challenges that shook her confidence in herself and affected her play. A severe shoulder inflammation reduced the effectiveness of her serves, and other injuries hampered her performance on the court. The death of a good friend to cancer that year also caused great emotional pain.

rusty from the time off, Maria lost in the fourth round of the Pacific Life Open, a tournament she had won the year before.

Determined to participate in the French Open that May, Maria faced her fear of needles and received a painful cortisone shot to treat her inflamed shoulder. But the tournament gave her trouble, anyway.

During a fourth-round match against Patty Schnyder of Switzerland, a fan shouted just as Maria served. Distracted, Schnyder lifted her hand to indicate she wasn't ready, but Maria's serve had already landed. The umpire didn't replay the point, and Maria didn't offer. For the rest of the match, the public jeered Maria for what was seen as poor sportsmanship. Maria appeared unaffected by the boos and heckling, but she looked tearful after she won. She advanced to the quarterfinals before being eliminated in the semifinals by Ana Ivanovic of Serbia.

⟫ EMOTIONAL CHALLENGES ⟪

Maria also suffered an emotional blow when she lost a friend to cancer. She had grown close to Jane Joyce, her coach's mother, and watched her battle ovarian cancer for six years. When Jane passed away that April, Maria and Michael suffered a difficult loss.

In addition to dealing with emotional pain, Maria continued to struggle with her physical injuries. She had been scheduled to play with the Russian team in the Federation Cup—an annual team competition in women's tennis sponsored by the International Tennis Federation. But her lingering injuries forced her to pull out of the first round in April and the semifinals in July. Russia made it to the finals, but because Maria hadn't played in the semifinals, the team captain declared her ineligible to compete. That decision hurt her chances of playing for Russia in the 2008 Olympics because participants must come from Russia's Fed Cup team.

But the lowest point of the season for Maria occurred in September, at the U.S. Open. There, her hopes of another Grand Slam title unraveled early, when she lost in the third round to 18-year-old Agnieszka Radwanska of Poland. The pain in Maria's shoulder was noticeable during the match. She committed 12 double faults on her serve and made 49 **unforced errors**.

During the second half of 2007, injuries forced Maria to compete in just six events. However, she managed to end a frustrating season on a high note. At the WTA Championships, in Madrid, Spain, she advanced to the final and nearly defeated the number one player, Justine Henin, 5-7, 7-5, 6-3. Maria's strong comeback impressed her former trainer, Robert Lansdorp. He predicted big victories for her in 2008.

➤ HELPING OTHERS ➤

While dealing with her own problems, Maria also had the desire to help others. In 2006, she had founded the Maria Sharapova Foundation, a charity to help at-risk children. She raised money for the foundation by auctioning off some of her tennis dresses at her Web site. And in 2007, she hosted a fund-raising auction with the car company Land Rover.

At La Costa Resort, in Carlsbad, California, children from Belarus present Maria with a painting of her dog, Dolce, on July 30, 2007. The children were brought to visit the United States by the Children of Chernobyl Foundation, an organization supported by Maria. She has also donated funds for other programs that help people living in the Chernobyl region.

In January 2007, in an effort to help prevent heat illness in children, Maria launched a global campaign in partnership with the sports drink company Gatorade. Called Beat the Heat: Play Safe, the program seeks to educate parents about how children playing sports in hot weather can be susceptible to dehydration.

The following February, Maria was appointed Goodwill Ambassador for the United Nations Development Program (UNDP). At the same time, she announced that the Maria Sharapova Foundation was donating $100,000 to help with UNDP projects in regions affected by the Chernobyl nuclear power plant disaster—Belarus, the Ukraine, and the Russian Federation. On April 26, 2007, at a UNDP event recognizing the anniversary of the tragedy, Sharapova said:

CROSS-CURRENTS

To learn how the international community has responded to the victims of the Chernobyl accident, read "Chernobyl Nuclear Disaster Aftermath." Go to page 55. ▶▶

> **❝I think there are two important things in life that helped me once, and young people living in the Chernobyl territories today need them badly too. They are self-confidence and opportunities to fulfill their potential.❞**

Maria shows what she's made of in this January 24, 2008, photo of her taken during her semifinal game against Jelena Jankovic at the Australian Open. She defeated her opponent quickly, by a score of 6-3, 6-1. After a tough 2007, Maria had spent the off-season practicing hard so she could perform at her best in 2008.

5

Looking to the Future

THE YEAR 2008 OFFERED A FRESH START FOR Maria. She was determined to shake off the frustrations of the past year when injuries had plagued her. The media had reported her inconsistencies and struggles, highlighting her difficult past season and the fact that the former number one player had clinched only two Grand Slam titles.

Maria refused to let the past year erode her confidence. Now she increased the intensity of her practices, hitting the courts early in the morning, breaking for lunch, and then continuing her workout.

⇒ THE WILL TO WIN ⇐

In early January, Maria readied herself for the 2008 season by playing two pre-season exhibition tournaments in Asia. In Singapore, she took on fellow Russian Anna Chakvetadze. Maria had defeated her the past seven times the two competed. Now she beat Chakvetadze for an eighth time. Next, Maria traveled to Hong Kong, China, where she lost in the sweltering heat to Venus Williams, Serena's sister.

Following the exhibition matches, Maria took a week off to rest and train for the first Grand Slam event of the year—the Australian Open. Typically, the hot summer sun baking the tennis courts in Melbourne presented an added challenge for Maria. This year, however, the courts had been resurfaced with a new material that would retain less heat.

Maria also readied herself for the Australian Open in another way. She was well known for her love of fashion and for her innovative tennis outfits. When she won the U.S. Open in 2006, she was wearing a short black tennis dress that she helped design. For her Australian Open appearance, Maria launched a new line of tennis apparel that she had designed with Nike. The dresses, visors, and bags featured splashy floral colors inspired by Australia and were made from a specially designed fabric that helped keep her cool.

⇒ ANOTHER GRAND SLAM TITLE ⇐

Although her shoulder was still fragile and the weather was hot—reaching over 93°F—Maria successfully battled her way to the top at the Australian Open. And she faced some of the world's toughest players. She beat Lindsay Davenport to make it into the quarterfinals. There, she challenged Justine Henin, the world's number one player, who had won her past 32 matches. In what some would say was one of the best matches Maria has ever played, she defeated Henin, 6-4, 6-0.

In the semifinal, Maria faced Jelena Jankovic of Serbia. Jankovic had won three of the four matches the two had recently played. But Maria swiftly defeated her opponent, advancing to the final, where she challenged Ana Ivanovic.

In the final match, Maria played a powerful game, with her serve acting as a highly accurate weapon. In about an hour and a half, she defeated Ivanovic. After a year of injuries and self-doubt, Maria had won her third Grand Slam title.

At the end of the game, Maria dropped to her knees in relief and joy. Later, in her speech to the crowd, Maria dedicated the victory to Michael Joyce's mother, Jane, who had inspired her:

"Every single day, every single time when we went on the court, Jane was the word that came into our

minds. I just gained a whole new perspective on life and my injuries and how to treat life with respect. **"**

At the same time, Maria also thanked another famous tennis star for her support. Billie Jean King had believed in Maria's ability to defeat the top ranked players in the tournament to win. Maria explained:

On January 26, 2008, Maria earned her third Grand Slam title by beating Ana Ivanovic, 7-5, 6-3. After dealing with so many problems the previous year, she admitted that the win overwhelmed her: "If I would have thought then that I'd be standing on that stage [today], with that winning trophy, I don't think I would have believed it."

"This morning I got a text from Billie Jean King saying, 'Champions take chances' and 'Pressure is a privilege.' And I think as an athlete that's what Ana and I and everyone who plays wants to achieve. We all want to take our chances, and I'm just so fortunate I took mine today."

Maria signs autographs for fans attending the 2008 Australian Open Tennis Championships, held in Melbourne. Her stellar performance at the Grand Slam event showed that despite her difficulties in 2007, she still had the passion, mental determination, and competitive edge needed to be the best in women's professional tennis.

⟫ MARIA AND HER FATHER ⟪

After Maria's Grand Slam event win, however, more scrutiny fell upon Yuri Sharapov. Warned in the past for coaching Maria during matches, he was widely criticized for his behavior at the end of Maria's quarterfinal match against Henin. Yuri had yanked the hood of his camouflage jacket over his head, looked at Maria, and made a throat-slashing motion. People saw his action as being directed towards Henin, and were outraged at the behavior.

Yuri later explained that he had meant no harm and that the gesture was unrelated to his daughter's opponent. Maria told reporters it was a private joke between the two of them. She had told her father that he looked like a criminal in his camouflage jacket. Weary of the criticism, Maria said that she wanted her father to get rid of the jacket.

Over the years, Yuri has been criticized for pushing too hard and exhibiting on-court behavior that goes too far. He has been accused of cursing, calling out to disrupt play, punching his fists into the air, and gesturing during matches. Many people say that his behavior does little to help Maria win, and that it actually undermines her achievements. They believe her victories come from her years of dedication and practice, not from on-court coaching.

⟫ TACKLING 2008 ⟪

With the Australian Open win, Maria's season was off to a strong start. In an interview with a group of reporters, she described her feelings about her third Grand Slam:

> **❝This is like success the second time around, and it's actually a lot sweeter. Because I think I've proven to myself that I can come back from having setbacks and negative thoughts and having doubts in my mind.❞**

In February, Maria traveled to Israel for the first time. For the 2008 Federation Cup event, Russia was playing host country Israel in the quarterfinal, and she was a member of Russia's team. The Russians were defending their title as

CROSS-CURRENTS

To find out how Maria feels about representing her home country on the court, read "Playing for Russia." Go to page 56. ▶▶

reigning champions, having defeated Italy in September 2007 to win the Fed Cup event.

In her first match, in Ramat Hasharon, Maria defeated Tzipi Oblizer, 6-0, 6-4. Next, in a ten-game winning streak, she beat Shahar Peer, 6-1, 6-1. Cheered on by Russian fans, Maria had helped Russia advance to the semifinals scheduled for April against the United States.

At the end of February, Maria headed to the Qatar Total Open, where she had triumphed in 2005. There, in a little over an hour, she defeated Russian Vera Zvonareva in the final. Continuing her perfect season, Maria claimed her second title of 2008.

Next, Maria flew to the neighboring country of the United Arab Emirates, where she planned to compete in the Dubai Tennis Championships. Now ranked number five in the world, Maria hoped to defeat Justine Henin, who stood at number one. Unfortunately, before the competition began, Maria had to withdraw because of a virus. With little rest and feeling ill, she felt unable to play the tournament's five matches.

Maria competed next at the Pacific Life Open in Indian Wells, California, where she had won in 2006. After winning her first 18 matches of the season, she lost in the semifinals to Svetlana Kuznetsova.

⇒ WHAT'S NEXT? ⇐

In April 2008, Maria turned 21 years old. The same month, she moved up to number three in the WTA world rankings. In the past seven years that she has played professional tennis, Maria has faced and defeated the best competitors from around the world. She has won numerous championship titles, including three Grand Slams—Wimbledon, the U.S. Open, and the Australian Open.

Maria has also won numerous awards for her skill on the court. In addition to her WTA awards, she has been named by the sports television channel ESPN as the ESPY Best Female Tennis Player in 2005 and in 2007. She was also named the ESPY Best International Athlete in 2007.

Achieving a fourth Grand Slam—the French Open—remains a goal for Maria. Although playing on the red clay surface has never been easy for her because of her style of play, she is determined to win the one Grand Slam event that she had not captured. Once she wins the French Open, she will have achieved what professional tennis players refer to as a "Career Grand Slam."

In January 2008 the official sponsor of the Women's Tennis Association tour—Sony Ericsson—signed Maria Sharapova to a multimillion-dollar four-year sponsorship deal as a global brand ambassador. In addition to promoting mobile phones and accessories, Maria is also involved in the design of various products made by Sony Ericsson such as cases, bags, and wallets.

⧽ HANDLING CELEBRITY ⧼

Her combination of talent, athleticism, and good looks has ensured that Maria remains in the spotlight for years to come. The sports superstar can be seen on numerous television entertainment and

In 2007 Maria, along with a Pomeranian dog that looked like her own pet, appeared in an advertising campaign for Canon in promoting one of the company's digital cameras. The campaign featured Maria and her pet's look-alike in television commercials, in print ads that were published in various high-profile consumer magazines, and on the Internet.

sports shows, as well as in television commercials. The products she endorses range from mobile phones to wristwatches to cameras to handbags and jewelry, not to mention tennis rackets, shoes, and clothing. In the beginning of 2008, Maria signed a four-year deal with mobile handset vendor Sony Ericsson. The company has also been the official sponsor of the WTA Tour since 2005.

According to the April 2008 issue of *Forbes* magazine, endorsement agreements with Maria's 11 sponsors earned the tennis superstar an estimated $23 million in 2007. *Forbes* has ranked her number one on its list of top-earning female athletes.

⇒ A TRUE CHAMPION ⇐

Maria has had a great impact on the world of tennis, setting new levels of skill and influencing thousands of young athletes by promoting the sport she loves. Tough, focused, and powerful on the court, Maria uses criticism to fuel her drive to succeed. After difficult losses, she pushes herself even harder. While people sometimes disapprove of her intensity, it has helped her to dominate the game.

Maria's successes off the court are impressive as well. She looks beyond her own achievements and tries to help others in need. Through her foundation, she donates both time and money to help at-risk children. And she has used her celebrity status to bring attention to programs that work to alleviate poverty in Russia as well as the rest of the world.

In the past few years, the Maria has grown and developed a new perspective on life in the world of tennis and beyond. She says:

> **"I've always said I wanted to be a champion on and off the court and when I mean champion I don't just mean winning tournaments. A champion is someone that respects people, acknowledges tough circumstances, and accepts defeats."**

Throughout her life, Maria Sharapova has faced challenges and dedicated her life to being the best she can at her sport. She is living her life doing what she loves, and the future holds much promise for her.

The Women's Tennis Association

Established in 1973, the Women's Tennis Association is the main organizing body for women's tennis. The WTA organizes professional women's tennis tournaments that are part of the WTA Tour. Players compete for prize money at 59 events held around the world.

The competitions include the end of season championships, or WTA Tour Championships, which feature the top-ranked players. The WTA also organizes numerous Tier tournaments, ranging from Tier I through Tier IV, which vary in prize money awarded and ability of players. Tier I tournaments are held throughout the year at locations around the world, including Berlin, Germany; Doha, Qatar; Tokyo, Japan; and Indian Wells, California, and Miami, Florida, in the United States.

The WTA gives "round points" that are based on players' performances at individual rounds of tournaments. That point total is used on a weekly basis in establishing a world ranking for each player.

World ranking differs from seeding, which is used to establish which players are matched up in tournaments. Seeding in a competition is based on past ranking and past performance on various court surfaces. Top seeds play against lower seeded or unseeded opponents in the early rounds of a competition.

(Go back to page 6.)

Maria speaks at a Sony Ericsson WTA Tour press conference. Phone manufacturer Sony Ericsson has sponsored the Women's Tennis Association Tour since 2005. Men professional tennis players compete and are ranked according to their performances in tournaments organized by the Association of Tennis Professionals, or the ATP.

Grand Slam Tournaments

Professional tennis players compete in many tournaments each year. But four tourneys, known as the Grand Slam events, are the most famous. Organized by the International Tennis Federation (ITF), which is the world governing body of tennis, these events are the Australian Open, the French Open, Wimbledon, and the U.S. Open.

Each tournament is played on a different type of surface. Every January, the world's best players compete on synthetic rubber courts in the Australian Open in Melbourne, Australia. In the spring, they face off at the French Open in Paris on red clay courts. In July, they play at Wimbledon in London on grassy lawn courts.

In September they compete at the U.S. Open in New York on green hard courts.

Each surface the players compete on has its own smell, color, and feel. The ball also bounces differently. Most courts in the United States are hard courts. A soft red clay court absorbs more of the ball's bounce so the game is slower. The clay can be dusty and slippery. On a grass court, the balls tend to skid and bounce low. On synthetic rubber courts, the game is slower than on grass, but faster than on clay. Players prefer different surfaces depending on the style of their game.

(Go back to page 6.)

Disaster in Russia

Before dawn on April 26, 1986, an explosion at the Chernobyl nuclear power plant in the Soviet Union, in today's country of Ukraine, caused the worst nuclear accident the world had ever seen. The plant produced energy from nuclear fission, or the splitting of atoms of enriched uranium. During the process, huge amounts of energy are released in the form of heat and radiation. The heat produced by fission is used to generate electricity used in homes and businesses.

In most countries, the fission process occurs in a reactor located in a reinforced concrete shell, which keeps radiation from being released into the atmosphere. However, the Chernobyl power plant reactors did not have this kind of containment structure.

The immense explosion in one of the plant's four reactors sent tons of radioactive debris into the atmosphere. Winds carried radiation contamination thousands of miles, but fallout was most extensive in the Soviet Republics of Ukraine and Belarus, and Russia's Bryansk region.

The Soviet government did not immediately tell people to leave the region around Chernobyl. Eventually, more than 350,000 people were evacuated from nearby towns. The government also distributed pills thought to lessen the effects of radiation. The Chernobyl disaster caused health, economic, social, and environmental problems costing billions of dollars.

(Go back to page 11.)

On the Court

All tennis courts are 78 feet (23.77 meters) long, and have a net that is about three feet high across the middle. When one person is playing on each side of the net, the court is 27 feet (8.23 meters) wide. This is called a singles match. When two-person teams are playing each other, the court is 36 feet (10.92 meters) wide. This is called a doubles match.

On each side of the net are two rectangular areas called service boxes. The boundaries on the ends of the court are called the baselines. The boundaries on the sides of the court are known as the sidelines.

Playing Tennis

To play a singles match in tennis, players start on opposite sides of the net. One player stands behind the baseline and serves. She tosses the ball up and hits it overhand with a racket over the net. The ball cannot touch the net and must land in the service box diagonally opposite from the server. If the ball doesn't drop into the service box, it is a **fault**. If the ball hits the box, the other player, or receiver, must try to return the shot before it bounces twice. If the receiver returns the ball to the server's court and it falls inbounds, the server must hit it back. When players alternate hitting the ball back and forth across the net, it is called a rally.

Scoring the Game

The server earns a point by hitting a shot that the receiver cannot return, without hitting the ball out of bounds or into the net. If the server misses the service box twice, she has made a **double fault**, and the receiver wins a point. When one player fails to make a legal return, the other player receives a point. In tennis, points are referred to in the following way: zero points are called "love," the first point is 15, the second is 30, and the third is 40.

The server continues to serve until one player has won at least four points, and has at least two points more than her opponent. This means the player has won a game. Players alternate service in playing more games. After winning at least six games (or sometimes more, because a player must win two more games than her opponent), the player is said to have won a set. The first person to win two sets takes the match.

(Go back to page 14.)

Tennis Greats

Throughout the years, many women have made great achievements on the tennis court. Three of the most famous women's tennis players are Billie Jean King and Chris Evert of the United States, and Martina Navratilova of the Czech Republic.

Daring, athletic, and determined, Billie Jean King (1943–), was a leader in women's tennis. She helped establish the Women's Tennis Association and acted as its first president in 1974. She achieved an impressive record during her professional tennis career, winning 39 Grand Slam titles (singles, women's doubles, and mixed doubles), and becoming the fifth woman to win all four Grand Slam singles events.

Known for her grace and strategy, Chris Evert (1954–) won nearly 90 percent of her matches, the best record of any professional tennis player in history. She captured at least one Grand Slam title for 13 consecutive years, and stood for five years as the world's top female player.

Famed for her style of attack and acrobatics on the court, Martina Navratilova (1956–) won 18 Grand Slam singles titles. During the 1980s, she set records for winning the most matches (1,500), tournaments (167), and matches in a row (74). Many people consider her to be the greatest female tennis player in history.

(Go back to page 20.)

A pioneer in women's professional tennis, King was involved in the founding of the Virginia Slims Tour, the Women's Tennis Association, the Women's Sports Foundation, and World Team Tennis. Maria has a personal relationship with the tennis great, noting "She's always a person who texts me if I have a tough moment or a great win."

Aches and Pains

Athletes in most sports suffer from aches and pains from time to time. They put tremendous stress on their bodies with intense practices and fierce competitions. Although they know to take care of themselves by resting and eating healthy foods, injuries can occur.

Tennis injuries range from blisters to severe problems requiring surgery. Athletes sometimes suffer from cramps in their arms, backs, and legs. They can strain tired muscles, and feel sick if they don't drink enough water when exercising. Running on hard tennis courts can mean that a player's knees, ankles, and back take a pounding. On soft courts, a player may hit more balls during the game and can have arm and shoulder problems. Ankle sprains, a common tennis injury, happen when a player's ankle twists or rolls to the outside. Other serious injuries occur when a player tears tendons, the tissues

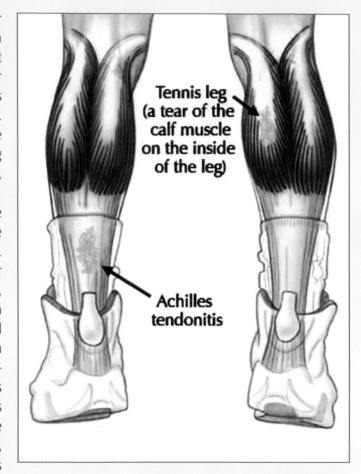

Achilles tendonitis is a painful and often debilitating inflammation of the tendon that is located in the back of the ankle. The inflammation causes pain over the back of the heel. Tennis leg is a severe burning pain in the calf of the leg. It is caused by a tear of the muscles and tendon portion of the calf muscle.

attaching the muscles to bones. Doctors sometimes treat an athlete's injuries with cortisone, a powerful drug that reduces swelling.

Both professional and amateur athletes use a method nicknamed RICE to sooth

injuries. R stands for rest. I means putting ice on the injury. C stands for compression, or bandaging the area. E stands for elevation, or putting the injured part up on a pillow.

(Go back to page 29.)

Chernobyl Nuclear Disaster Aftermath

More than two decades after the explosion at the Chernobyl nuclear power plant, the people who live in the surrounding regions still face problems. Following the accident, more than 350,000 people evacuated from the surrounding region. However about 5.5 million remained.

Radioactive Contamination

The greatest radioactive contamination occurred in a 19-mile (30-km) zone surrounding the Chernobyl nuclear power plant. The radioactivity killed surrounding pine forests that were bulldozed over in cleanup efforts. The villages in this area were evacuated. They remain empty of people today, although the immediate region around the power plant has become a sanctuary for some wildlife.

Although some officials believe the contamination is no longer a danger in the rest of the area affected by the disaster, some organizations disagree. They believe that thousands will eventually die from cancers caused by exposure to high levels of radiation. Some people living in the region suffer health problems ranging from infections to different types of cancer. Many children in areas surrounding Chernobyl have developed thyroid cancer, a disease that is rare in other parts of the world.

Concerns over exposure to radiation and its possible effect on their health have caused many people living in Belarus, Ukraine, and other parts of Russia to have high levels of stress, emotional difficulties, and poor health. Many of them live in poverty and don't have access to good health care.

Chernobyl Recovery Project

The United Nations, an international organization of countries that addresses worldwide issues, is leading a recovery project to help people living in regions affected by the Chernobyl accident. The programs hope to provide new jobs, improve local facilities, and offer programs to help people deal with their fears regarding radiation exposure. Some of the community development programs aim to improve public areas by planting gardens and building community sports fields. Others provide funding to local hospitals.

Maria is aiding the Chernobyl recovery project by serving as a UNDP Goodwill Ambassador. The job involves making public service announcements and participating in activities to bring attention to the needs of people living in poor areas. She and the Maria Sharapova Foundation have donated funds to support eight youth-oriented UNDP projects that will establish computer centers, schools, sports facilities, and family hospitals. All of the programs are designed to help improve the physical and mental well-being of children and their families so that their lives can change for the better.

(Go back to page 39.) ◄◄

Playing for Russia

Although Maria has trained and lived in the United States for many years, she is still a Russian citizen and proud of her **heritage**. In a 2003 interview on the WTA Tour Web site, she explains:

❝I'm very proud to represent my country. I know that I have spent a lot of time in the U.S. to train for my tennis, but my heart is Russian, and all my family still live in Russia. It's very important to me—being Russian.❞

From a young age, Maria learned about the Russian culture from her mother. Although Maria's travels throughout the world have given her the opportunity to sample many different kinds of foods, she prefers Russian dishes. Borscht, a Russian beet soup served hot with sour cream, is an especial favorite.

Maria has also told reporters that she has long dreamed of representing her country at the Olympics. As a young girl, she says, she remembers watching the Russian women's team practice in Moscow. Because she has played on the Russian Federation Cup team she is eligible for the Russian Olympics team.

Maria (left) joins Anna Chakvetadze (center) and Elena Vesnina in celebrating Russia's victory over Italy at the final for the 2007 Federation Cup, held on September 16, 2007. Because she had not played in previous Fed Cup games, Maria was not on the Russian team in the final. However, she played for Russia in the 2008 Fed Cup event.

(Go back to page 45.)

1987 Maria Sharapova is born on April 19 in Nyagan, Russia.

1989 The Sharapov family moves to Sochi, Russia.

1991 After receiving a hand-me-down racket, Maria begins to play tennis.

1993 At a tennis clinic in Moscow, tennis star Martina Navratilova recommends that Maria train professionally.

1994 Maria and her father move to Florida in March.

1995 At age nine, Maria begins training begins at the Bollettieri Tennis Academy in Bradenton, Florida.

1996 Following a long separation, Maria and her mother Yelena are reunited in June.

1998 Maria begins training with tennis coach Robert Lansdorp, and signs an endorsement deal with Nike.

2001 Fourteen-year-old Maria turns pro in April.

2002 Maria becomes the youngest player to reach the finals of the Australian Junior Open Championship. She signs an endorsement deal with Prince.

2003 Maria wins the Japan Open in October, and donates a portion of her winnings to charity. At the end of the year, she is ranked number 32 in the world.

2004 At age 17, Maria wins Wimbledon in July and the Japan Open in October. That November, she wins the WTA Championships.

2005 In August, Maria becomes the first female Russian player to be ranked number one in the world. She wins the Qatar Total Open and the Pan Pacific Open, and travels to Moscow to play in the Kremlin Cup.

2006 In January, Maria injures her ankle and withdraws from play for two months. In September, she wins the U.S. Open. She takes championship titles in the Pacific Life Open, the Acura Classic, and the Zurich Open. In August, she founds the Maria Sharapova Foundation.

2007 As Maria struggles with injuries, she is defeated in January at the Australian Open and early in other tournaments. In February, she is named a U.N. Goodwill Ambassador.

2008 In January, Maria wins the Australia Open, and in April is ranked third in the world. She represents Russia in the quarterfinals of the Federation Cup, held in Israel in February.

Career Statistics

Year	Wins	Earnings	Highest Ranking Achieved
2002	3	$23,000	(186)
2003	5	$222,005	(32)
2004	6	$2,529,977	(4)
2005	3	$1,821,283	(1)
2006	5	$3,674,501	(2)
2007	1	$1,758,550	(1)
2008*	3	$1,760,626	(3)
Total	25	$11,992,028	

*Through April 2008

Selected Awards

2003   WTA Newcomer of the Year

2004   WTA Tour Player of the Year
WTA Most Improved Player of the Year

2005   ESPY Best Female Tennis Player

2006   Whirlpool 6th Sense Player of the Year

2007   ESPY Best Female Tennis Player
ESPY Best International Female Athlete

2008   United States Sports Academy Athlete of the Month, January

Books

Antoun, Rob. *Women's Tennis Tactics*. Champaign, IL: Human Kinetics Publishers, 2007.

Guillermo-Newton, Judith. *Competitive Tennis for Girls*. New York: Rosen Publishing Group, 2002.

Matsuzaki, Carol. *Tennis Fundamentals*. Champaign, IL: Human Kinetics, 2004.

Savage, Jeff. *Maria Sharapova*. Minneapolis, MN: First Avenue Editions, 2008.

Williams, Pat. *How to Be Like Women Athletes of Influence: 32 Women at the Top of Their Game and How You Can Get There Too*. Deerfield Beach, FL: Health Communications, Inc., 2007.

Williams, Venus. *How to Play Tennis*. New York: DK Publishing, 2004.

Web Sites

http://www.sonyericssonwtatour.com

The official Web site of the WTA offers news items, descriptions of tournaments, player profiles and blogs, as well as tennis tips.

http://www.mariasharapova.com

The official Web site for Maria Sharapova provides a short biography, her career statistics and accomplishments, recent news, and a forum for readers to ask Maria questions.

http://www.usta.com

The United States Tennis Association has acted as the national governing body of tennis in the United States since 1881. Its Web site includes information about tennis rules, tips on how to play, and video clips of different players.

http://www.itftennis.com

The official Web site of the International Tennis Federation provides a history of tennis, links to official Web sites for each of the four Grand Slam events, and a radio page that offers news from recent tournaments.

http://www.cofcsd.org

The Web site for The Children of Chernobyl Foundation gives information about Maria Sharapova's charity work as a sponsor for the foundation and as a United Nations Goodwill Ambassador.

Publisher's note:

The Web sites mentioned in this book were active at the time of publication. The publisher is not responsible for Web sites that have changed their addresses or discontinued operation since the date of publication. The publisher will review and update the Web site addresses each time the book is reprinted.

backhand—a stroke in tennis when the player hits the ball with the back of the hand turned forward.

double fault—two faults in a row; as a result, server loses a point.

doubles—a tennis game played by four players, with two on each side of the court.

endorse—to give public support to a product either by advertising, using a product, or talking about it.

fault—a serve that fails to put the ball in the correct area of play.

forehand—a stroke in tennis when the player hits the ball with the palm of the hand turned forward.

forfeit—to give up a game to the opponent, often because of injury or illness.

Grand Slam event—one of the four most prestigious and important tennis championships each year. Tennis's Grand Slam events are the Australian Open, in January; the French Open, in May; Wimbledon, in July; and the U.S. Open, in September.

heritage—cultural traditions handed down from a person's ancestors.

opponent—a person competing or playing against you in a sport or game.

scholarship—money awarded to a student to help pay the costs of his or her education.

seed—ranking within a specific tournament.

serve—a stroke in tennis when a player hits the ball to the opponent to start the game.

singles—a tennis game played by two players.

sponsor—a company that pays a person to support and promote its product publicly.

sportsmanship—the treatment of another player with fairness and courtesy.

tournament—a sports event made up of a series of games in which many athletes compete.

unforced error—when a player has time to get the ball back in play but fails to do so because of a mistake.

page 6 "She is extremely strict . . ." Boeck, Greg, "Russian's Game a Thing of Beauty," *USA Today*, January 12, 2004.

page 8 "It's a little early . . ." Ibid.

page 8 "All that has happened . . ." Clarey, Christopher, "Sharapova Conquers Wimbledon," *New York Times*, July 4, 2004.

page 12 "In those days . . ." Frankland, Neil, "Sharapova Shares Personal Childhood Memories After Reaching Australian Final," *Associated Press Sports*, January 24, 2008. http://www.msnbc.com.

page 14 "None of the things . . ." Lansdorp, Robert, "Making Maria," *Tennis*, May 2004, pp. 42–27.

page 17 "I definitely feel . . ." Boeck, "Russian's Game a Thing of Beauty."

page 19 "I don't love it . . ." Connors, Claire. "Grand Slam's Golden Girl," *Shape*, September 2007.

page 20 "I never . . ." Clarey, "Sharapova Conquers Wimbledon."

page 23 "There are definitely . . ." Drucker, Joel, "Solving Maria," *Tennis*, May 2007, pp. 46–51.

page 27 "Maria has this . . ." Robbins, Liz, "Sometimes Sharapova's Father Can Be Her Biggest Distraction," *New York Times*, September 9, 2005.

page 30 "As long as . . ." Macur, Juliet, "Recuperating Sharapova Leads a Russian Advance," *New York Times*, May 31, 2007, p. D5.

page 33 "When you go . . ." Robbins, Liz, "Title is the Strongest Endorsement," *New York Times*, September 10, 2006.

page 34 "I believe . . ." Ibid.

page 35 "You can never . . ." Clarey, Christopher, "Williams Shocks Sharapova to Win in Australia," *New York Times*, January 27, 2007.

page 39 "I think . . ." United Nations Development Program, "Ban Ki-moon and Maria Sharapova Commemorate Chernobyl Tragedy," *United Nations Development Program official Web site*, April 26, 2007. http://www.undp.org/goodwill/sharapova.

page 42 "Every single day . . ." Clarey, Christopher, "With Third Title, Sharapova Shows She's Back," *New York Times*, January 26, 2008.

page 44 "This morning . . ." Ibid.

page 45 "This is like . . ." Clarey, Christopher, "A Second Wave of Success Is Sweeter for Sharapova," *New York Times*, January 27, 2008.

page 49 "I've always said . . ." Maria Sharapova's official Web site, "Ask Maria," March 10, 2008. http://www.MariaSharapova.com

page 56 "I'm very proud . . ." Sony Ericsson WTA Tour official Web site, " Getting to Know Maria Sharapova," June 16, 2003. http://www.sonyericssonwtatour.com

Kerrily Sapet is the author of several books and magazine articles for young adults. She lives in Oswego, Illinois, with her husband, Jason, and their son, Ben.

PICTURE CREDITS

page

1: Jillian Edelstein/Camera Press
4: Nike/NMI
7: Abaca Press/KRT
9: Dave Caulkin/AP Photo
10: ASP Library
13: New Millennium Images
15: ASP Library
16: ASP Library
18: SportsChrome Pix
21: TAG Heuer/NMI
22: Frederic J. Brown/AFP/Getty Images
25: Clive Brunskill/Getty Images
26: Hiromasa Mano/AFP/Getty Images
28: Rob Griffith/AP Photo
31: Cancan Chu/Getty Images

32: Matthew Stockman/Getty Images
33: Don Emmert/AFP/Getty Images
35: Nike/PRMS
36: Nike/PRMS
38: John Cordes/Icon SMI
40: Clive Brunskill/Getty Images
43: Quinn Rooney/Getty Images
44: Mark Dadswell/Getty Images
47: Sony Ericsson/PRMS
48: Nike/PRMS
50: Stephen Dunn/Getty Images
53: Mirrorpix Photos
54: MedVision
56: Ivan Sekretarev/AP Photo

Front cover: Nike/NMI